AF572231

SLOW LORIS POETRY SERIES

I WOULD ALSO LIKE TO MENTION ALUMINUM: *Poems and a Conversation*
William Stafford, edited by William Heyen

THE END OF THE ICE AGE, Ed Ochester

WAKING UP, LATE, Gary Eddy

THE ANIMAL IN THE BUSH: *Poems on Poetry,* David Ignatow
edited by Patrick Carey

ROAD ENDS AT TAHOLA, Richard Hugo

TUNING, Jane Bailey

SONGS OF AUTUMN, Sigitas Geda, translated from the Lithuanian
in a bilingual edition by Jonas Zdanys

GREEN IN THE BODY, Robert Winner

POLAR SUN, Sandi Piccione

OBLIQUE LIGHT, Lynn Emanuel

INTERSTATE, Marie Harris

FORTHCOMING

FATHER IS A PILLOW TIED TO A BROOM, Gary Soto

HEART, GRAIN, Nils Nelson

THE ANCIENT WARS, Paul Zimmer

INTERSTATE

INTERSTATE

Marie Harris

for Charlie — a belated signature (9/9[illegible]) with love, Marie

SLOW LORIS PRESS
Pittsburgh

I would like to thank the editors of the magazines in which versions of these poems originally appeared: *Blacksmith I & II; Truck; Poetry NOW; Aspect; Maine Edition; Conch; Epoch; Parnassus: Poetry in Review; Longhouse; Out of Sight; Lamp in the Spine; Penumbra; Handbook.* I would also like to acknowledge the publication of sections of *Interstate* in the *Ardis Anthology of New American Poetry,* and the New England Anthology from *Choomia.*

And to my friends in the Alice James Poetry Cooperative, thanks for permission to reprint versions of some of the sections from RAW HONEY.

In the "my sons" poem, the epigraph is taken from *There Are Two Lives* (Simon & Schuster, 1970), edited by Richard Lewis.

Cover photograph and design by Charter Weeks

Printed in the United States of America
Hoechstetter Printing Company
Pittsburgh, Pennsylvania

First Printing, February, 1980

Library of Congress Cataloging in Publication Data
Harris, Marie.
Interstate.

(Slow Loris poetry series)
I. Title. II. Series.
PS3558.A6475157 811'.5'4 79-25366
ISBN 0-918366-18-6
ISBN 0-918366-17-8 pbk.

SLOW LORIS PRESS
923 Highview Street
Pittsburgh, Pennsylvania 15206

for Charter Weeks, at the end of the trip

INTERSTATE

*****

the form occurs repeatedly
as a function of growth in plants and animals:
the ratio
in the chambered spirals, interstate
the arrangement of seeds in the sunflower
the pine cone
                    you make the irrational proportion

egg
chicken
egg
home
leaving home
home

*****

leaving Ithaca: Buttermilk Falls
or the deep pool in Six Mile Creek where I swam,
shedding an indoor day with my shirt and jeans
squatting naked on the warm rocks with a few friends

leaving Ithaca with the children north to Toronto
(north on I-89, west on 90
to Buffalo and across an international boundary
where even the names of the hamburger stands don't
change)

three of us and our essentials
tape recorder full of music
2000 baseball trading cards
hiking boots and sweaters
typewriter

you learn
what to carry with you

aboard CNRR coach
settled and moving
out of Toronto, I imagine
hands at every smudged window
knocking for my attention
writing on the dusty glass
"Don't go! It's the same
everywhere."
pole by pole
we gather speed

north by Georgian Bay turning dark . . . Sudbury
west to the Soo
                                        we sleep sitting up
                                        slumped on each other
Thunder Bay

Kenora: Irish fog rising off the lakes
look way out the window, see the end of the train
emerging from a forest, the engine ahead entering one

Manitoba

Winnipeg at midnight
like any station at midnight
chocolate bars and magazines
standing on one foot, then the other
wondering about Winnipeg
or

Regina
Moose Jaw
Swift Current
morning approaching Medicine Hat, Alberta

crossed the whole continent
carrying the children like saddlebags
                                        when I dashed off the train
                                        for fresh bread and cheese
                                        they hung out the window, yelling
                                        as the conductor announced the minutes
                                        till departure   schooled in departures
                                        we learn to count backwards

Calgary, Alberta, Canada
                    south on Rt 2 by car to Fort McLeod
                    west on Rt 3 over Crow's Nest Pass
                    B.C. to Fernie

(stopped for a few minutes at the Frank Slide
where did all that rock come from
so fast
what does it take to bury a town
                    instantly)

TO: my next sister's home
FROM: Ithaca, Buttermilk Falls and the deep pool
  in Six Mile Creek
where I swam, shedding a day of late, indoor spring
squatting naked with a few friends

TO: Annie, my next sister
FROM: Ithaca, Buttermilk Falls
a marriage of ten years

we make space for each other, pushing aside
a half-finished peanut butter and jelly sandwich,
a pile of newspaper, layer on layer

to Annie for a month in the Canadian Rockies
(the sky is a foggy weight-belt on the Three Sisters
rain, like a mud boot on the valley
the bush is rain and river)

dear Annie

*****

we are encysted in shiny cocoons
collecting windshield stickers
from parking lots and town dumps

we are postcards
a forwarding address
our speech is clipped
and the grocer begins to know us

*****

ice has locked the steering mechanism
glare ice locks the pavement in black

I watch myself barrel north
watch the mountains widening
in the rear view mirror

behind the wheel, I believe I am in control
I make the road diminish behind me
make it disappear into a point
not unlike a taillight

*****

time is distorted the way it is
on days when winter moves through the intestines
raining in weepy spasms

I shuttle back and forth over the same bridge
on the same dime

my eyes are too tired to hold the road
I sleep fitfully in a Savarin parking lot
dreaming that pieces of my life are pulling away
like trucks

*****

you imagined the lover
I will never be   I am
so sorry

tripping on the hem of it
falling backward
into the bottomless apology
I am so sorry

fog shreds the edges of the horned moon
the road home
is a short memory
I reinvent ahead of the lowbeams

*****

the children travel best at night
sleep through the New Jersey Turnpike
through the detours, the silent construction
through the night smells and neon
around pink cities
under pale pink and yellow skies:
the semidark of the east coast

the lights of tollbooths and truckstops
flicker on their faces

*****

we lived with our mistakes
17 miles to the next exit
we have never heard such silences

each headlight cut the fog at a different angle
thin clouds arranged themselves against a giant moon
in the image of a fish skeleton

staying awake
Gethsemane

the missed exit
another accident in the accidents
of our lives together

REST AREA
in which, clean, machined, 24 hr
we might
at another time
rest

*****

the street of schools
the street of the fishing cat
the street of the innocents
the square of the risen bread
the street of kites and ducklings

maple ave
state street
front street

we are not within walking distance

*****

I-495 avoids Boston
starts up the tiny NH coast another road

THERE ARE NO SERVICES ON THIS ROUTE

the sand is crusty and salt whips off the rocks
at Hampton Beach
empty tide pools
footprints that remain like fingerprints
when dough has risen

I carry you with me reluctantly
inside old books
in the prints at the corners of my eyes
in the pout of my son's mouth
                                        this death
                                        is organic: life's mulch: dead
                                        love
starting out
late at night
knowing just that
I will avoid Boston

*****

. . . we went up in the mountains and we found silver ore
and other rocks and bullit shells . . . we are having a ball . . .
guess what—by mistake I put my hand on a cactus and
guess what—I came up with 20 quills in my hand. But luckely
I was smart enough to get them out with a nail clippers
and also I fixed my glove all by myself!

the first time we talked about divorce
was in the south
when they were babies
                                        you take this one &
                                        I'll take that one
                                        and I'll be in Scotland . . .

the goat turns in circles
the duck disappeared
the goose sat on her eggs until they rotted

                                        I am missing something

*****

the sails strain out from the bent mast
kelp drifts on sea-soil, the salt
dries into maps on my arms

I walk by the edge of the highway
my hair stiff with salt

barefooted, dragging shreds of seaweed and frayed rope
a dry anchor
I look among the chicory for soil
in which to plant

*****

he hears it in his temples
like surf behind fog
the same beat
the same pebbles and shells grinding
another cubic inch of sand
for the same beach
every year the orange rose hips
the children
the damp jigsaws

my father with his kite
fishing without a hook in the jetstream
for silence

*****

we leave dried layers of ourselves
in schoolyards and empty rooms
the skins are patterned
they can be read like snakeskin
a severed tree
a caterpillar
a riverbed

the molt is one kind of record
transparencies to hold up to the light

sometimes it's all we have left
the stiff skin
of friendships

*****

the ties loosen like shoelaces
drag along the ground
develop knots
catch in bicycle wheels

*****

Mother
we are of an age.
We have had done with babies.
Neither of us will ever again
smell sour at the shoulder
measure liquids carefully
sing and sing
rock with fatigue
repeat the rhythms of sleep
sleep sleep.

I left you in the doorway
of my wedding
waving a monogrammed towel.

Now my boys
are gone away
too soon.
Too soon, you say.
They are necessary
pieces in my puzzle family,
the sons
of my first
careless daughter.

Come here, you say to them,
come home.

*****

out of gas
along the sinews of empire
somewhere between White River Junction
and Concord

the car runs on lunar energy
playing continuous music of the spheres
the shades of hit-and-run victims rise
off the shoulders of the road

> a doe with old scars
> unborn fawns
> possums with tails curled around silver bumpers
> racoons with radiator grilles for faces
> millions of butterflies, mosquitos, ladybugs
> preserved in radial perfection like ferns in shale

bits of paper emblazoned with golden arches
flutter in the breakdown lane
the battery fills with rainwater
mushrooms come and go on the carpet
moles nest in the back seat and eat it

the stationary car
the stopped wave

I hunt for missing parts
a feathered pouch lies beside the car
containing fingernail parings and baby teeth

*****

the completion of the stretch
of I-93
between here and the border
is in doubt

I am camped in the shadow of the earth
movers

*****

the detour led to the foot of Blue Job Mt.

the neighbors' sons
helped me heft my belongings
into his kitchen
smiled when I talked

about chickens and goats
Ball jars and a screened porch
insulation for his leaky walls
and the airborne attic

*****

summer

mosquitos breed in standing water

I have not moved
in a year

animals and vegetables surround me
like a fence

peas scale the chicken wire
pale soldiers

I am a rocking chair
a lap robe

settled

like the tree broken along the wall
the stone placed by a shoulder of frost
the house rocking on the hill like a boat

*****

I follow the shadow of my car
past tight white yankee houses
hardwood stacked between trees
testifies to a summer
unlike the one I spent

half a pig in the freezer
I pace the kitchen

what has altered
the pitch of my friendships

*****

the hurricane
moves to the northeast

September rain
days of it
for nothing
nothing needs water

the dirt roads are slick with storm
and the leaves glow

he will never leave me
even though today he wants
something warm and dry

*****

I am slowing into the cidercold
learning the limits
of latitude

*****

like homing pigeons with iridescent necks
they find me

a small iron pot tracks me to every stove
the fat Japanese kettle boils all waters
keeping inside it the stain
of each deep earth I have made into tea
I can't lose the glass ashtray
the wooden bowl surfaces, flotsam from the wreck
of my stubborn marriage

the window frosts over into its own white landscape
and I pull the quilt that followed me from Connecticut Hill
around my shoulders

*****

out of habit I preserve nothing
as though winter will freeze
what I need: the green apples on their branches
carrots in the ground
the rattled notes of the guinea fowl

or—winter will freeze the things
I need: oil
in the lumbering car
the road away from here

*****

instead of stacking apple and split oak
or clearing what snow will bury
instead of mulching the ragged garden
protecting mock orange
grape vine, thyme,

I pack books like winter hay
choose which houseplants to take
which lamps

I will remember,
build
one day
from notes scratched on envelopes
and memories in my hands,
from information stored in attics and barns
and the trunks of dying cars,
accounts passed by word of mouth
from clippings

the house that will hold all of us: children
lovers, family, neighbors, animals

*****

The goat comes to me in a dream of families.
I bring her hay and grain and water warmed against
the March air, pull the first, thick, yellow milk
from under her until it flows in hot quarts into the pail.

. . . my breasts are swollen. I don't know how; *the baby is frantic*
for food and my body will not let down. My son tastes salt in his milk,
hears a new pulse, cries and sucks.

Head at her flank, listening to her complicated digestion
move like unfamiliar scales, I bring down the milk: thumb
and forefinger circled at the top of the teat to stop the flow
backward into the udder, sucking down with three fingers
and palm. I squat in the hay of her stall,
listening.

. . . he pushes at me. I give him more. He sings in his sleep.

After the last milk squirts into the pail, there is more.
Nudge the udder. There is more and it is the sweetest
and richest. Strip out the milk and the goat will give more
next time. Strip her dry.

. . . I wake to his need. Crying brings me out of sleep; crying
pulls me out of half-finished dreams. I am reluctant. My milk is sour.

It's early. I am milking the goat and looking at the maple
red with spring. It's early. I am nursing the baby and looking out
gray windows. The letters of my name are spelled in milk. Milk
is the perfume I wear.

The letters of my name spell a constellation.
No one will set a course by any of its stars.

*****

my days lose shape
and that is spring

or I am lost

I am lost
near home

he saw me start off with a basket
now it's full of mushrooms
white angels
red angels

I should have told him I meant to leave
by the woods

*****

in the barn the goat stalls are empty
the pine boards exhale their ghosts
chaff filters down spider silk

the factory of the year
shuts down

*****

another place

pigeons putter by a curb
and herring gulls, starlings,
some kind of city sparrow

just a yard full of chickens
mallard, white china geese

I am not rooted
but anchored, like a tug
in fog

it's not too late to begin again
this time I will make a life
solitary as a night-hunting bird
useless as an earring

*****

jaw fused like thermalpane glass
heart soft and out of condition
I am not prepared

for your house
with the equilibrium of a painting
turned upside down

your broccoli and pork
your banked fire

not prepared
by another single moment
for you

I am flying
and staying put
like a tree

*****

cattails
boneset
fields of goldenrod
elderberry
wild mints

the food and the remedy
the decoration

*****

I am seeing things

the undersides of leaves
lit by the river
splinters of fish
the berries of last spring's trillium
full of winter

seeing things clearly

your face

*****

The highway runs across the pools
where the seaweeds grow.
Everybody likes the highway
but it's made a crack
between the ocean
and my father
and my mind.

Suyama Sadae, age 10

my sons,
you heard the highway
in my pulse
you were powerless
you were passengers

it's an old Indian trick,
my friend used to say:
walking backwards in the snow

you have learned to walk back
wearing a path of memory
to every house

sentences ran on for two or three years
before they broke
into new paragraphs of location

your speech is inflected
rich with geographies

* * * * *

there was not enough
I sent you from my table

don't come home
nothing will grow here
the land will turn
to juniper and berry thickets

grow up

* * * * *

on this quiet road the news arrives slowly
from all the places I have sent you
and when it comes the words are smudged

it is raining

I won't hear of it
for years

* * * * *

the kitchen is lit with lanterns
votive candles of grape jam
peach butter
cider wine in green bottles

this is the kitchen light
fueled by years of anger

come home now
the wick burns clean

visit in my kitchen
I will be your grandmother

*****

last summer I planted packets of defeated corn
wilting beets
lettuce that would not head
vulnerable squash
an envelope of nasturtiums labeled:
Losing Heart, Leggy

I will never feel comfortable with gardens
men or children

my seasons of success
I attribute to the weather
or the moon
and so will always find your love
an amazement
an unexpected bounty of parsley

*****

At a deepening
of the Isinglass River
I lie down in stones and tea-colored water.
I think: be careful. Do not say
home. The bones
of that word mend slowly.

Marie Harris is the author of *Raw Honey* from AliceJamesBooks. She lives in New Hampshire.

Interstate, in the Slow Loris Press series of books, has been published by Anthony and Patricia Petrosky on February 15, 1980. Publication of this book was made possible by a grant from the National Endowment for the Arts.